45623
The Tiger Shark

Brad Burnham
AR B.L.: 4.6
Points: 0.5

DATE DUE

the TiGeR shark

Brad Burnham

The Rosen Publishing Group's
PowerKids Press™
New York

For Bos

Published in 2001 by The Rosen Publishing Group, Inc.
29 East 21st Street, New York, NY 10010

First Edition

Book Design: Maria Melendez

Photo Credits: Cover, title page, © Bettmann/CORBIS; pp. 2, 3, 8, 9, 22, 23, 24 © Animals, Animals; pp. 4, 5, 7, 8, 10, 11, 12, 14, 16, 17, 18, 19, 20, 21 © Peter Arnold; pp. 8, 12, 13, 15, 16 © Digital Stock; p. 15 © Innerspace Visions.

Burnham, Brad.
    The tiger shark / Brad Burnham.
        p. cm.— (The underwater world of sharks)
    Includes index.
    Summary: This book introduces the physical characteristics, behavior, habitat, and life cycle of the tiger shark.
    ISBN 0-8239-5586-9
    1. Tiger shark—Juvenile literature. [1. Tiger shark. 2. Sharks.] I. Title. II. Series.
    2000
    597.3—dc21

Manufactured in the United States of America

Contents

1 Meet the Tiger Shark   5

2 Tropical Swimmer   6

3 Hunting on the Coast   9

4 Bent Teeth   10

5 A Swimming Garbage Can   13

6 Dozens of Babies   14

7 Finding Prey   17

8 Preparing to Bite   18

9 Tiger Shark Attacks   21

10 In Our Lives   22

Glossary   23

Index   24

Web Sites   24

Meet the TIGER SHARK

Tiger sharks are big sharks. They can grow to be up to 18 feet (5.5 m) long. They can weigh up to 2,000 pounds (907 kg). Many sharks have pointed **snouts**. Tiger sharks do not. They have a snout that is squared off in front.

Tiger sharks are grayish in color. Their bellies are a lighter color. Tiger sharks have dark stripes on their backs when they are young. The stripes look like the stripes on a tiger. Tiger sharks were given their name because of these tigerlike stripes. The stripes fade as the sharks get older. The scientific name for tiger sharks is *Galeocerdo cuvieri*.

◄ Tiger sharks get their name because of the dark, tigerlike stripes they have on their backs when they are young.

Tropical SWIMMER

Tiger sharks live in **tropical** waters all over the world. They live in the warmer parts of the Pacific, Atlantic, and Indian Oceans. Tiger sharks are the most common kind of large shark found in the waters of the Caribbean and the Gulf of Mexico.

Some tiger sharks **migrate** from one place to another during the year. In the summer, tiger sharks in the Atlantic Ocean swim north along the eastern coast of the United States. The sharks swim back to tropical waters when the water on the eastern coast gets too cold.

Tiger sharks prefer tropical waters. One place that tiger sharks can be found is the Gulf of Mexico. ▶

GULF OF
MEXICO

HUNTING on the Coast

Tiger sharks are **predators**. Predators are animals that hunt other animals for food. Tiger sharks hunt for food near the shore. Water can be up to 30 feet (9.1 m) deep close to the shore. Tiger sharks even swim in water that is only a few feet (meters) deep. One tiger shark was seen chasing a type of fish called a stingray in very **shallow** water.

Tiger sharks hunt in different kinds of water **environments**. A **coral reef** is a good place for tiger sharks to hunt for **prey**. Prey are animals that are hunted for food. Tiger sharks also hunt for prey at the **mouths** of rivers.

◄ *The picture on the far left is of a stingray. Tiger sharks hunt stingrays for food.*

Bent TEETH

Tiger sharks have teeth that are good for grabbing and cutting. Their teeth are bent at the tip. The tip of each tooth is bent back toward the inside of the tiger shark's mouth. The bend in each tooth helps a tiger shark hold on to its prey. Prey cannot pull away from a tiger shark's mouth. The teeth sink deeper into the skin when the prey tries to get free.

The edge of each tiger shark tooth is thin and sharp. There are also small bumps on each tooth, which make a **serrated** edge. The serrated edge is very good for cutting through meat and bone.

A tiger shark's teeth can even cut through bone! This is because the teeth have serrated edges that work like the edges of a saw. ▶

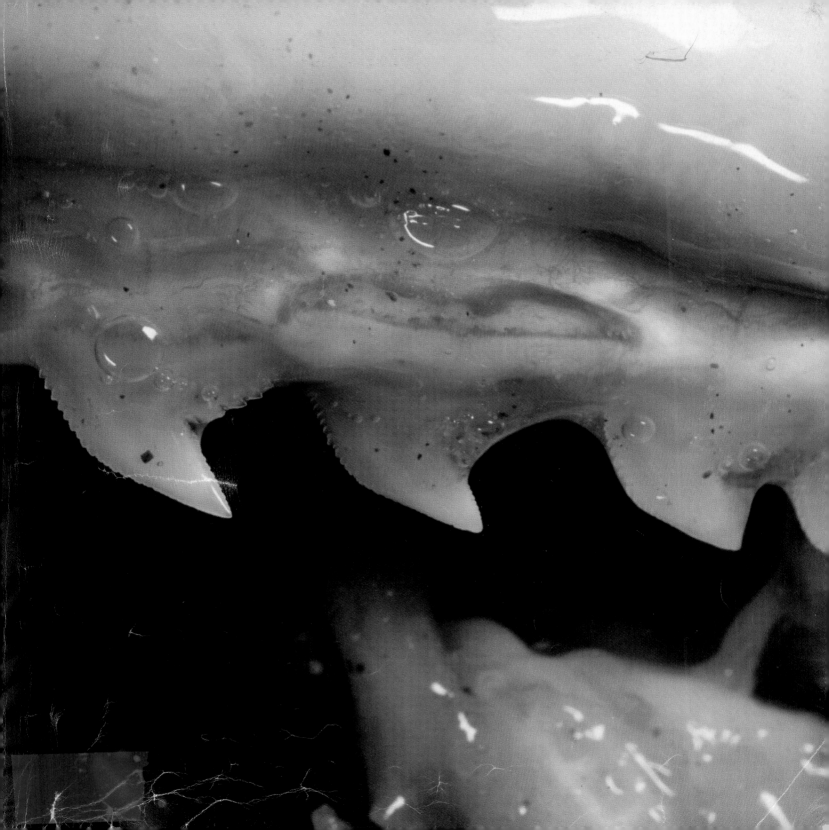

A Swimming GARBAGE Can

Tiger sharks eat almost anything that will fit into their mouths. They eat many kinds of ocean animals, including squid, octopuses, lobsters, sea lions, and all sorts of fish. They also eat other sharks. One tiger shark caught off the coast of North Carolina had 11 pieces of shark meat in its stomach. The pieces of meat were from three different **species** of sharks.

Tiger sharks also eat other things besides ocean animals. People have found a leather wallet, a huge coil of copper wire, beer bottles, a bag of potatoes, and a can of green peas inside the stomachs of different tiger sharks. People have even found pieces of metal **armor** inside a tiger shark!

◀ *Tiger sharks are not fussy eaters. They eat many ocean animals, including octopuses like the one shown in this picture.*

Dozens of BABIES

A female tiger shark usually gives birth to between 30 and 40 babies. These babies are called **pups**. No other kind of shark gives birth to more pups at one time.

Some sharks lay **fertilized eggs** in the water. Tiger sharks do not lay their eggs. They keep the fertilized eggs inside their bodies. Some of the eggs develop into pups. The pups eat any eggs that have not been fertilized. After about nine months, the mother gives birth to her pups. The pups are able to take care of themselves as soon as they are born.

Tiger shark pups are between 20 and 30 inches (50.8 and 76.2 cm) long when they are born. ▶

Finding PREY

Tiger sharks do not always need to see their prey to find it. They may first notice a sound. Tiger sharks can hear the sound of a fish struggling on a fishing line after it has been caught. Some sharks can hear these sounds from as far away as a quarter of a mile (.402 m).

Tiger sharks that are hunting can sense smells from as far away as 100 yards (91.4 m). That's about the length of a football field. Tiger sharks can sense a small drop of blood in a large amount of water. They can also sense **vibrations**. Tiger sharks have what are known as **lateral lines**. Lateral lines are small tunnels that run down both sides of a shark's body. They help sharks sense the small movements of fish in the ocean.

◄ *Tiger sharks use their lateral lines to sense the vibrations of their prey. These small tunnels help them track the prey more easily.*

H.C. STORM SCHOOL

17

Preparing to BITE

There are at least two things that happen before tiger sharks bite their prey. First they close their third eyelid. Most sharks have only an upper and a lower eyelid on each eye. Tiger sharks have a third eyelid that covers the entire eye. This eyelid protects the eye from prey as the tiger shark tries to get close enough to take a bite. Tiger sharks do a second thing before biting prey. They **extend** their jaws so they are in a better position to bite down on large animals. These two things give tiger sharks the ability to attack many different kinds of prey.

Tiger sharks extend their jaws before biting prey. This makes it easier for them to bite down on large animals. ▶

Tiger Shark ATTACKS

Tiger sharks are one of the four sharks that are considered to be the most dangerous to people. The three other most dangerous sharks are the great white shark, the bull shark, and the oceanic whitetip.

In India and Australia, tiger sharks have been blamed for many attacks on people. In the West Indies, tiger sharks are the most feared of all the sharks. Tiger sharks are feared in the United States, too. One man was killed by a tiger shark in Hawaii while surfing. In Florida, two tiger sharks caught off the coast had human body parts in their stomachs.

◄ *Tiger sharks, along with great whites, bull sharks, and oceanic whitetips, are considered very dangerous sharks. Still, only 5 to 10 people are killed as a result of shark attacks each year.*

In Our LIVES

Tiger sharks are important beyond the ocean, too. During World War II, a group of American pilots was formed. This group helped defend China, which was one of America's **allies**, against Japan. The pilots painted tiger shark jaws on the noses of their airplanes. The image of the shark was meant to make their enemies afraid. This became their symbol and they were known as the Flying Tigers. Native Hawaiians believe tiger sharks represent the god called Aumakua. It is clear that all around the world these dangerous but beautiful sharks play an important part in people's lives.

Glossary

allies (AH-lyz) Groups of people that agree to help another group of people.

armor (AR-mer) A type of uniform used in battle to protect the body.

coral reef (KOR-ul REEF) A chain of coral where many ocean creatures live.

environments (en-VY-urn-ments) All the living things and conditions that make up a place.

extend (ek-STEND) To stretch out.

fertilized eggs (FUR-til-eyzd EHGZ) Eggs that can develop into babies.

Galeocerdo cuvieri (gal-ee-oh-CER-do KU-ver-i) The scientific name for tiger sharks.

lateral lines (LAT-er-ul LYNZ) A line of small canals along the back of the shark that can sense the movement of fish.

migrate (MY-grayt) When large groups of animals or people move from one place to another.

mouths (MOWTHZ) The parts of rivers where water flows into larger bodies of water.

predators (PREH-duh-terz) Animals that kill other animals for food.

prey (PRAY) An animal that is eaten by another animal for food.

pups (PUPS) A type of baby animal.

serrated (SER-rayt-ed) To have teeth-like points at the end.

shallow (SHA-low) Not deep.

snouts (SNOWTS) Parts of animal heads that include the nose, mouth, and jaw.

species (SPEE-sheez) A group of living things that have certain basic things in common.

tropical (TRAH-pih-kul) An area that is very hot and humid all year round.

vibrations (vy-BRAY-shunz) Motions that can be felt through cloud, air, or water.

Index

A
attack, 18, 21

B
babies, 14

E
eggs, 14
eyelid, 18

F
fish, 9, 13, 17
Flying Tigers, 22

H
hunt, 9, 17

J
jaws, 18, 22

M
migrate, 6

P
people, 13, 21, 22
predators, 9
prey, 9, 10, 17, 18

S
sense, 17
snouts, 5
stomach, 13, 21
stripes, 5

T
teeth, 10

Web Sites

To learn more about tiger sharks, check out these Web sites:
http://www.mote.org
http://www.pbs.org/wgbh/nova/sharks/world/whoswho.html